The New Inequality

NEW DEMOCRACY FORUM

The New Inequality

CREATING SOLUTIONS
FOR POOR AMERICA

Richard B. Freeman

Foreword by ROBERT B. REICH

Edited by Joshua Cohen and Joel Rogers
for *Boston Review*

BEACON PRESS

BOSTON

BEACON PRESS
25 Beacon Street
Boston, Massachusetts 02108-2892
www.beacon.org

Beacon Press books are published under the auspices of the
Unitarian Universalist Association of Congregations.

04 03 02 01 00 99   8 7 6 5 4 3 2 1

This book is printed on recycled acid-free paper that contains at least 20
percent postconsumer waste and meets the uncoated paper ANSI/NISO
specifications for permanence as revised in 1992.

Text design by Christopher Kuntze
Composition by Wilsted & Taylor Publishing Services

Library of Congress Cataloging-in-Publication Data
    Freeman, Richard B. (Richard Barry), 1943–
        The new inequality : creating solutions for poor America / Richard B.
    Freeman ; foreword by Robert B. Reich ; edited by Joshua Cohen and Joel
    Rogers for Boston review.
            p.   cm. — (The new democracy forum)
        ISBN 0-8070-4435-0 (pbk.)
            1. Income distribution—United States.   2. Poor—United States.
    3. Wealth—United States.   4. Equality—United States.   5. Economic
    assistance, Domestic—United States.   I. Cohen, Joshua, 1951–   .
    II. Rogers, Joel, 1952–   .   III. Title.   IV. Series.
    HC110.I5F74   1999
    3—dc21   98-37374

Contents

III

Foreword

ROBERT B. REICH

*W*hen I was asked to write this foreword, the American economy was on a roll: unemployment low, inflation almost nonexistent, solid growth, a stock market surging merrily into the stratosphere. Even inequality, the subject of this book, appeared to have been somewhat tamed. Incomes at the bottom were rising, in part because the minimum wage had recently been raised but also because jobs were so plentiful that people at or near the bottom were working longer hours, and because in certain geographic areas employers were so hard put to find employees that they were willing to pay more. Some commentators had the temerity to proclaim this a "new economy," immune to the old business cycle. They were wrong, of course. And by the time you read this, all may have collapsed.

But whatever the apparent benefits of the economic boom, a fundamental problem remains. Behind the business cycles lies a two-decade-long trend toward widening inequality of wages, of fringe benefits like pensions and health care, and of wealth. It is a *new* inequality—hence the title of this book—in two senses. First, between 1940 and the late 1970s, the trend had been in the other direction, toward greater equality. What's been happening since then is indeed new. Second, the new trend is connected to deep changes in the structure of our economy, involving rapid and widespread adaptation of new technologies and an equally rapid shift toward global production.

We are becoming a two-tiered society. In the top, an expanding number of well-educated managerial, professional, and technical workers who spend most of their days identifying and solving problems—often utilizing new computer technologies—and sell their symbolic and analytic insights to an ever-widening market, often spanning the globe. In the bottom, an expanding number of relatively poorly educated women and men who provide an array of in-person services—retail, restaurant, hospital, custodial, child care, elder care, security, and other forms of tending.

Should you care? If the poorer members of our society were gaining only a bit of ground while the richer were gaining far more, you might still have cause for concern. Even though everyone was doing better, inequality would be widening. After a point, the bonds that kept our society together would snap. Every decision we tried to arrive at together—about trade, immigration, education, taxes, and social insurance (health, welfare, retirement), or whatever—would almost be impossible to make, because it would have such differing consequences for the relatively rich than for the relatively poor, and we could no longer draw upon a common reservoir of trust and agreed-upon norms to deal with such differences. We would begin to lose our capacity for democratic governance; we would forfeit the moral authority that defined us as a nation.

But even if you were willing to accept such a dire consequence as the price for improving everyone's standard of living, you would not accept what's been happening. The economy has grown, inequality has widened, and the poorer members of our society have been *losing* ground.

America is now richer than it has been at any time in its history—as measured by our domestic product divided by the number of our people, or by our total net worth divided by the number of our people. We are richer than any other nation in the world—richer, by far, than any nation in the history of the world. And yet a significant portion of our population has become poorer over the last two decades. And behind the business cycle, the trend continues.

This is the biggest economic and social—and, perhaps, moral—challenge we face as a society. And yet there is remarkably little public discussion about it. That you have chosen to pick up this book and have read this far into it puts you, by definition, in a rather small group whose members are at least interested. Why isn't everyone?

America is overwhelmingly optimistic, practical, and innovative when it comes to solving big problems. We win world wars. We clean up the environment. We tackle AIDS. We're also pretty good at changing our ways when the status quo seems unfair. We embrace the cause of civil rights, we open workplace doors to women and the disabled. But the trend toward inequality, coupled with declining living standards for so many of our people, is somehow more difficult for us to comprehend. It has happened gradually. The business cycle masks some of it. Its root causes are more difficult to see.

For those of us on the more comfortable side of the widening divide, inequality *itself* is more difficult to see. Americans are segregating by income—into different towns, using different modes of transportation, employing different public facilities (parks, playgrounds, schools, libraries), and working and playing in different places. And the comfortable class includes most of the people who are in the business with communicating with everyone else—professional journalists, academicians, television producers, and—dare I say it?—most politicians. We don't see the problem and we don't hear about it, because we're living in a parallel universe which rarely, if ever, intersects with the people who are losing ground. And even if we happen to read about them in a book like this, they too often remain something of an abstraction.

For many years before I became secretary of labor in the first Clinton administration, I wrote about widening inequality (when it wasn't nearly as wide as it is now). I watched the numbers as they poured out of the Bureau of Labor Statistics and the Census, year after year. I thought I knew what was going on. After all, I had grown up in a family of modest means. My father had a small dress shop in a factory town in upper New York State. As a young man I had tutored inner-city kids. Surely I knew what was going on. But then, during my four years in office, I traveled around America. I visited poor and working-class communities, talked with hospital orderlies and child-care workers, met with farm workers and janitors, listened to garment workers and clerical workers, went into mines and telemarketing centers, heard from union rank-and-file, from poor single mothers on welfare, from poor single men moving from job to job. Before, I thought I knew what was going on, and in a sense I did. But I didn't really *know*.

The other thing I learned after four years as secretary of labor is that there's rarely a shortage of worthwhile ideas for how to solve a public problem, or at least good ideas to try out on a small scale in order to learn more about how they work in practice. Richard Freeman comes up with some important and intriguing possibilities in his essay. I agree with most of them, although I think he understates the central importance of improving education and training. Nonetheless, his list is an excellent starting place, and you'll find that it stimulates an interesting debate.

What's most lacking, I discovered, is political will to

implement worthwhile ideas, or even to try them. *Politics*. The term sounds messy and even a bit sordid these days. Who in their right mind would get involved in it? Let me tell you something. If you want to begin to tackle the problem of widening inequality, you've got to get politically active. I'm all in favor of volunteerism, a thousand points of light, a vigorous not-for-profit sector, and so on. But in the end, the long-term trend toward widening inequality won't turn around without a determined effort by a large number of people to make sure that enough resources get behind the right ideas. This requires a political movement.

During the last few years, politics has worked perversely: taxes on the wealthy have been cut, and so have programs directed at the poor. The reason isn't difficult to explain. Many Americans—especially those who have been losing ground—have given up on politics. As their incomes have sunk, they've lost confidence that the "system" will work in their interest. That cynicism has generated a self-fulfilling prophesy. Politicians stop paying attention to people who don't vote, who don't work the phone banks or walk the precincts, who have opted out. And the political inattention seems to justify the cynicism. Meanwhile, the top tier has experienced precisely the opposite—a virtuous cycle in which campaign contributions have attracted the rapt attention of politicians, the attention has elicited even more money, which in turn has given the top tier even greater influence.

Don't get me wrong. As individuals, many members of the comfortable class would be deeply concerned if they understood the nature and consequences of the new inequality. Many already do. But as participants in institutions committed either to preserving the status quo or gaining further economic advantage for their constituents—mutual funds, pension funds, publicly held corporations, trade associations, conservative foundations, and assorted business lobbies—their concern has been laundered out of the politics they indirectly pursue.

So, by all means read what follows. Debate it with your friends and colleagues. But then, resolve to do something about it. You don't have to run for president or become a cabinet officer (if you feel the urge, take an aspirin and a cold shower, then wait until it passes). Just get involved.

Editors' Preface

JOSHUA COHEN AND JOEL ROGERS

*T*he purpose of the New Democracy Forum is to foster honest, serious discussion of pressing national problems, and constructive debate about political solutions to them. Growing economic inequality in the United States is, in our view, the most pressing problem of domestic politics. So when we initiated the Forum in Fall 1996, we put inequality at the top of our list of topics.

Why does inequality matter so much? Some people object to inequality because it is bad for the economy; others claim that it corrodes the bonds of political community. We begin from the idea that our economy should be a fair system—designed to provide everyone with opportunities to contribute, and to ensure a reasonable life for all. It shouldn't be a talent contest, designed to reward those with unusual abilities, or a lottery in which luck determines fate. So we are not worried about all inequalities—that Bill Gates is richer than Warren Buffett, or that heart surgeons are compensated more handsomely than radiologists—but about those that are unfair.

For example, some people, simply by virtue of being

{ xv }

born wealthier or in a "better neighborhood," have better chances in life than others. They get a head start because of the accidents of social circumstance. In a society dedicated to the proposition that we all are created equal, what could possibly justify such inequalities of opportunity at the starting gate of life?

Or consider people in this society who are not doing well economically—working men and women who may lack the skills that now receive high rewards in the current economy, but who work hard, play fair, worry about their jobs, and love their children and want the best for them. For more than two decades, they have been rewarded with wage stagnation and decline. Surely, through smart, concerted collective action, their circumstances could be improved. And if they could be, it is plainly unfair, indeed insulting, not even to make the effort.

Similar ideas about unfair inequalities of opportunity and reward guide Richard Freeman's lead essay "Solving the New Inequality." When we put inequality at the top of our list of topics, we put Freeman at the top of the list of New Democracy Forum contributors. Freeman is the country's leading labor economist, and he combines the analytics, empirics, policy imagination, and moral decency required for provoking a wide-ranging debate about economic justice. In his essay, he advances a five-part proposal to promote economic fairness. The central idea is to ensure that we all enter the market on a more level playing field—with greater assets of capital, human and otherwise.

Any such complex proposal raises hard questions of economic fact and political possibility. Fully appreciating those complexities, Freeman advances his ideas in a tentative spirit. But he also understands the stakes. This is, as Freeman says, "probably the most important economic argument of our lifetimes." What we now need is to open the discussion—to fight the paralyzing idea that we can't correct gross inequality, and the corrupt idea that we shouldn't bother.

❦ I ❦

Solving the New Inequality

RICHARD B. FREEMAN

Over the past two decades, income inequality in the United States has increased massively. This jump owes to the unprecedentedly abysmal earnings experience of low-paid Americans, income stagnation covering about 80 percent of all families, and an increase in upper-end incomes. The rise in inequality—greater than in most other developed countries—has reversed the equalization in income and wealth we experienced between 1945 and 1970. The United States has now cemented its traditional position as the leader in inequality among advanced countries.[1]

These facts are not in dispute. From the Milliken Institute on the right to the Economic Policy Institute on the left, virtually all analysts agree that something has gone seriously awry with our income distribution. And absent some major national effort to change things, the new inequality is likely to continue (the recently reported 1996 decline in poverty and uptick in wages notwithstanding). The next recession will surely exacerbate it, and the forces contributing to wage losses at the bottom—foreign competition, immigration of low-skilled labor, technological changes, shifts from manufacturing to service industries, declining union density, subcontracting, and so on—are unlikely to reverse themselves anytime soon.

Falling or stagnating incomes for most workers and rising inequality threaten American ideals of political "classlessness" and shared citizenship. Left unattended, the new inequality threatens us with a two-tiered society—what I have elsewhere called an "apartheid economy"—in which the successful upper and upper-middle classes live lives fundamentally different from the working classes and the poor.[2] Such an economy will function well for substantial numbers, but will not meet our nation's democratic ideal of advancing the well-being of the average citizen. For many it promises the loss of the "American dream."

What should we do about the new inequality? That's the important question, but before getting to it I want to put two less fundamental ones to the side.

First, what are the causes of the new inequality? The short answer is that analysts disagree. Pat Buchanan and Ross Perot put immigration and trade at the top. The Clinton administration blames technology. Republicans blame taxes and government regulations. The AFL-CIO stresses declining unionism and the fall in the real value of the minimum wage. It would be nice to know how much each of these factors (and others) contribute to the problem. But such knowledge is largely irrelevant to the "what is to be done?" question that should be our principal concern. After all, determining what caused the new inequality does not dictate the policies we need to attack it. Technology may indeed be the culprit, for example, but that doesn't recommend destroying computers.

Second, what are the proximate effects of the new inequality? The short answer is that we don't know, because the new inequality is so new. Our prison population—to reach 3 percent of the male workforce by 2000 or so, surely a record for any democratic society—is largely composed of high school dropouts for whom the job market has collapsed, but no one knows how much the decline in the pay and employment of low-skill workers has contributed to criminal activities. Poorer Americans live shorter and less healthy lives than richer Americans, but just how much shorter and less healthy they have recently become as a result of labor market changes is hard to estimate. Intact families are strained by the increased inability of less-educated men to make a living, and child support payments are hard to dun from delinquent dads with no cash, but again, getting precise estimates of the effects is difficult.

As with cause, however, so with effect. We don't need precise estimates on the ill effects of inequality to agree that it is a serious problem. No one argues that we need more inequality to generate work effort or economic growth. To the contrary, most recent economic studies suggest that inequality is harmful to growth. So let's put aside causes and consequences and simply stipulate that the problem is real, big, and worth solving.

In what follows, I offer some candidate proposals on how to do that. I emphasize their "candidate" status. Excepting radio talk show hosts, nobody claims certainty about what new policies we need. And given our fundamental uncertainty about how the new economy works, nobody should. At this point of our knowledge, we should be more vigorous exploring alternative strategies than peddling answers. Since we cannot explore forever, and at some point need to plunk for some definite directions and policies, what we most need now is a free-for-all debate about what might be done. That debate should be disciplined by reason, but not cramped by political litmus tests or stringent feasibility assumptions. We're in new territory here, and today's impossibilities may turn out to be tomorrow's consensus solutions.

Consider my suggested strategies, then, as an invitation to that debate. I think they make sense—otherwise I wouldn't make them—but of course you may disagree. Don't leave it there, however. If you disagree, say why. And if you think you've got a better suggestion, get it on the table. Let the argument begin about how we as a nation might alleviate the new inequality that threatens us. It's probably the most important economic argument of our lifetimes.

THE NEW INEQUALITY AND POLICY FAILURE

Before getting to proposals, however, let's state a bit more precisely the dimensions of the problem—the facts about the new inequality that any knowledgeable economist, regardless of his or her political persuasion, would readily acknowledge as true—and say something about current policy discussion around them.

Here are the facts:

Income inequality has skyrocketed. In 1979, for example, on an hourly basis, the top decile of men earned four times what the bottom decile earned; by 1993 they were earning five times as much. This rise in inequality occurred in the context of general wage stagnation: the median male worker, for example, earns about 13 percent less than the median male 15 years ago—despite his being older and having more education.

Inequality in earnings has led to inequality in family incomes. Virtually all of the past decade's economic growth has gone to the upper 5 percent of families. Since the early 1970s, while the income of the top 1 percent of households has doubled, family and household incomes have stagnated or declined for 80 percent of the population.

Heavy income losses at the bottom of the distribution have resulted in increased poverty. The share of Americans living in poverty rose from 11.2 percent in 1974 to 15.1 percent in 1993, and the "poverty deficit"—or amount of money needed to lift all to the poverty line—doubled in real terms. The effects are felt most heavily among children. The lowest quintile of American children are now poorer than the lowest quintile of children in 15 other advanced countries, even as the upper quintile of American children are richer than the upper quintile in those same countries.

Measured in "purchasing power parity" terms (which take account of differences in prices), the bottom third of U.S. workers now earn less per hour than the bottom third of workers in Europe or Japan. Tenth decile German workers make about twice as much as tenth decile American workers, and the tenth decile worker in a typical European Union country makes 40 percent or so more than a tenth decile American—this without taking account of the fact that the European has national health insurance and other protections that the American either buys out of the paycheck or does without.

Across the board, high-skill groups—college graduates, professionals, managers, older workers—have obtained greater pay increases than low-skill groups. The pay of professional men, for instance, increased by 6 percent while that of laborers fell by 21 percent and that of machine operators fell by 16 percent. The only low-paid group whose wages increased were women whose pay rose relative to men (though there still remains a male-female pay gap).[3]

Falling incomes and rising inequality have occurred

despite U.S. success in generating jobs and a huge work effort by Americans. Since 1974, the U.S. employment/population ratio has grown from 65 percent to 71 percent while Organization of Economic Cooperation and Development (OECD) Europe's has fallen from 65 percent to 60 percent. Americans work considerably more hours and take less vacation than Europeans; according to the newest OECD data, we even work more than the Japanese.[4] The experience of prolonged earnings declines and rising inequality in the context of job growth and economic expansion is unprecedented in U.S. economic history.

If these are the uncontroverted facts, what's the policy response? At this point, from both major parties, next to nothing.

When it first came into power, the Clinton administration tackled the problem through increases in the Earned Income Tax Credit (EITC), a proposed national health insurance plan, and additional training programs. But the EITC doesn't address declining wages themselves, health insurance went nowhere, and training would have to be truly massive to make a dent in the problem. You don't correct a 20 percent downward trend in real earnings by providing a young person with a three- to six-month training program or by getting him or her a Graduate Equivalency Diploma.

The 1996 minimum wage increase did do something for workers at the bottom of the distribution, with, I surmise, little loss of employment. But the minimum remains low, and its recent increase was not part of any general plan to intervene at the low end of the labor market. It was forced on the Clinton administration by organized labor and massive public support: this is one redistribution three-quarters of Americans wanted. And the 1996 welfare "reform" will have a countervailing effect by increasing the market supply of less-skilled workers and downward pressure on their wages.

Properly configured, a cut in income taxes could do something. But Bob Dole's 1996 campaign pledge to give Americans a 15 percent cut—coupled as it was with promises to roll back the capital gains tax, maintain the reduced fiscal deficit, not cut military spending, and reduce taxes on Social Security income—seemed more campaign gimmick than serious redistributive policy.

Some argue that we can grow our way out of the problem through more relaxed Federal Reserve policies or tax spurs to capital investment. But while an expansionary Fed policy and increased capital investment (however spurred) would be welcome, and while faster growth would certainly ease any long-run solution, the experience of the last 15 years should seriously qualify any hope that growth alone will do it. We've had job growth and income has declined for many and been spread more unevenly.

Others argue that the problem will correct itself

through market forces. Faced with increased returns to schooling, more people will get themselves skilled, and the reduced supply of less-skilled workers will drive their wages up. Some of this market logic is working—enrollments in higher education are up—and the wages of college graduates have recently declined, but inequality is not returning to pre-1980s levels. What most troubles me about the "market-will-solve-this" view is that young people in the "baby bust" generation that followed the boomers have seen their pay fall despite a diminished supply of young people on the job market.

In sum, current "strategies" run the gamut from inadequate to sham. There is no reason to believe that they will solve the new inequality problem. So we're back to the question we started with: What should we do?

FIVE STRATEGIES FOR RAISING THE BOTTOM (AND RELIEVING INEQUALITY)

I have phrased the title to this section deliberately. I believe our goal should be to increase the earnings and living standards of those at the bottom—thereby diminishing inequality by improving their position relative to the better-off—rather than level down those who are prospering without lifting up the poor. As the AFL-CIO has recently argued, we want to give America a raise, with the biggest part going to low-paid workers.

The result will in fact be a substantial income redistribution from those who have gained so much in the past 15 to 20 years, not a redistribution for its own sake, but for its results in improving the living standards of those now at or near the bottom.

How to do this? Recognizing both the new economic circumstances and the successes and failures of the traditional welfare state, I would recommend five broad strategies of reform that would take us "out of the box" of conventional remedies and constitute radical reform, in the best sense:

1. Move redistributive strategies away from reliance on income transfers and toward the transfer of productive assets.

2. Shift redistribution forward in the life course, targeting interventions on the young.

3. Raise the "social wage" (guaranteed, nonmarket benefits for all citizens) while taxing it progressively.

4. Encourage the growth of those citizen organizations with the clearest stake in improving the position of low-wage workers—namely unions.

5. Target metropolitan regions as the building blocks of a more egalitarian economy.

In combination, pursuit of these strategies would substantially equalize economic opportunity, and institutionalize pressures for a more egalitarian income distribution, while improving living standards generally, hopefully in ways that are politically more acceptable than the present welfare state.

ASSET-BASED REDISTRIBUTION

One virtue of capitalism is that individuals have capital assets, physical and human, that they can freely use to the best of their ability and that earn them market returns. Decentralized markets permit this use in diverse circumstances, taking advantage of local knowledge and individual initiative. The "hard budget constraints" of market competition, moreover, assure that only "wise" (profit-generating) use is rewarded. The result is invention, productivity, and increased social wealth.

Of course, real-world capitalism doesn't correspond perfectly to this picture. Real markets are imperfectly competitive, and the operation of even perfectly competitive markets has some undesirable social consequences. For example, individuals with strong private economic positions use those positions politically to soften the "budget constraint" on their incompetence. Defense contractors are a prominent case in point, and the U.S. tax code is full of other examples.

Still, you get the basic idea. The really big problem in capitalism—at least from the perspective of those concerned about inequality—is that those original assets are themselves unequally distributed. If we were to start democratic capitalism with a blank slate, we would naturally divide the ownership of existing physical assets equally among the population (as the East Europeans and Russians have tried with their various privatization schemes). Give everyone a voucher to use for education or training or for investment in physical assets, and let them compete in the market. In this competition—by dint of ability or luck or effort—some people would become wealthy and others would become poor. For the latter, we'd want to build some sort of safety net. But this would be a distinctly secondary response. Our main strategy—be we left or right—for fighting income inequality under capitalism, should be to assure a fair initial distribution of physical and human capital themselves. Equality of income obtained in the first instance via greater equality in those assets, rather than as an after-the-fact (of earning or luck) state redistribution of income from rich to poor, would enable us to better square the circle of market efficiency and egalitarian aspiration.

Of course, we don't live in a virgin capitalism. In a functioning free-enterprise economy, no one could sensibly propose seizing private assets and redistributing them on an equal per capita basis. The modern welfare state has sought to alleviate inequality through more indirect means—by meliorating the effects of their exercise through redistributive income transfers. But that shouldn't keep us from drawing a lesson for designing a policy to fight the new equality from what we would do if we were starting anew. And at least at the margin, we could begin now to move toward such asset-based, rather than income-based, redistributive strategies.

Consider a two-step approach in this direction.

First, give workers themselves control of the most important assets they already "own" but do not control—the $5 trillion in deferred wages now residing in pension and other retirement funds. Amounting to nearly a third of all U.S. financial assets, this money could be used in ways that substantially reduce inequality. The same goes for the worker equity tied up in employee stock-option plans (ESOPs), which already claim some 11 million employee participants. We should amend current law (Taft-Hartley, ERISA, and the tax provisions around ESOPs themselves) to permit real worker control of worker assets.

Assume that worker-owners, no less than capitalists, use their assets to advance their interests. If labor's capital was more firmly under the control of its worker-owners, we would expect it would be used to help foreclose the "low road" on industrial restructuring that has disrupted American labor markets and depressed family incomes; to reduce domestic investment's sensitivity to speculative international capital flows; and to increase the will-

ingness of management to undertake policies that benefit a wider range of enterprise stakeholders than short-
term owners of shares. Each move would benefit the less-
well-off, though perhaps not the very poor. We would
also expect that a more "worker-friendly" portfolio of
national investment would include investment in metropolitan cores—where many workers with pension assets
reside and where their investment would bring the dou-
ble bounce of an income return and an improved community—and here it can be expected to benefit poor urban minority populations.[5] In addition, and of great
interest to the business community, such changes in capital accountability might increase the aggregate amount
of capital available for investment. This would have
positive effects on economic growth, and allow management to focus on long-run business problems, including
business strategies to improve the position of the worse-
off.

But there is no need to stop here. As a second and
longer-term step toward an asset-based egalitarian strategy, we should move toward more fundamental asset redistribution. Imagine if instead of being promised at
birth that you will get a Social Security pension decades
in the future (assuming taxpayers then are willing to
fund this obligation) you were given a trust fund based
on bonds or stocks whose returns would constitute your
social transfer. Such a fund would give citizens a share of

the nation's capital endowment similar to the privatization vouchers in the transitional economies. The incompetent poor would then be more like the incompetent rich: they would have income from assets that would let them live at some basic level, without depending on income transfers.

How might we fund such a redistribution and set up a citizen asset trust fund? Through progressive taxes, in part on inheritance and other forms of wealth, but also through the income tax, or some consumption or value-added tax. There are important design issues on which we would have to strike compromises in any such scheme. To prevent new cross-generational equity problems or perverse savings incentives, we might stipulate that only the income from the individual capital account could be consumed by its holder. Individuals might allot their trust fund investments in different ways (subject to some fiduciary responsibility limits). But the capital itself would, upon the holder's death, revert to the national pool for disbursement to the next round of babies.

All manner of critical details need to be worked out, of course, from the precise dimensions of such accounts and their funding, to the speed at which this sort of social funding base could supplement or supplant traditional entitlement programs. But as a general proposition, asset redistribution, coupled with the accountability-inducing possibilities of the market, makes more compelling sense in a society based on private capital than after-tax income transfer and insurance. Instead of demonizing welfare mothers, we'd all be tending our social stock portfolios—and so would they.

STARTING-GATE EQUALITY

If we should move at the margin from income to asset redistribution, we should also move at the margin from late-in-life redistribution to early-in-life. This doesn't mean taking Grandma's Social Security check away from her tomorrow (unless she is Grandma Moneybags). But as a share of total social expenditure, money spent on her grandchildren should substantially increase.

In terms of economic efficiency, all intuition is that early interventions—educational programs of diverse sorts (such as Head Start), programs to teach better parenting skills, increased resources for primary schooling—are more effective than later interventions.[6] But even if they are not, we still have good reason to favor them. Redistributive efforts focused on the young rather than on the old may be less distorting of savings, because unconditional benefits to the old adversely affect savings behavior and work effort.

Whatever their other problems, European welfare states—with child allowances in tax codes, parental leaves, various forms of subsidies for day care, and, increasingly, more substantial and more equal spending on education[7]—have done a better job in ensuring "starting-gate" equality for children.

Most Americans would, I believe, prefer generating equality "naturally," from more equal labor-market endowments, to generating it "unnaturally" by correcting market outcomes through taxes and transfers. If that could be done, egalitarian policies would have a more stable base. To do it, however, we of course need to invest in people before they reach those labor markets.

Moving on this goal would, of course, be a hugely expensive proposition. We'd need things like full insurance and counseling on prenatal and maternal care; paid time off at birth for either parent (which would encourage both work and the two-parent family); health insurance for the child up to maturity; child-care subsidies sufficient to get all kids into safe and responsible care by qualified caregivers earning a living wage; child allowances to keep all kids out of poverty; and increased investment in schooling such as intensive and extensive use of technology, more teacher training and more demanding standards on teacher performance, and an extension of the school year.

How much might all this cost? Another $200 billion a year? It would be a "Marshall Plan" for the poorest among us—our nation's children—and an investment in our future. Properly developed, no economic strategy is more likely to excite popular imagination, bring us together as a nation, or reverse the new inequality than a massive investment in starting-gate equality for children.

Like asset redistribution, shifting social expenditures forward in the life cycle fits with the broad goal of remaking America as the land of equal opportunity within a market economy. Indeed, just as asset redistribution is an effort to level the playing field by providing capital resources to those without such, starting-gate equality is an effort to level the field by providing educational or human capital resources to them as well. These strategies are the same approach applied to different aspects of the inequality problem. The effect of both would be to raise living standards of the least well-off.

A HIGHER SOCIAL WAGE, PROGRESSIVELY TAXED

Any scheme to address the problems of the current poor, including the working poor, and of those who even in an ideal future will run into economic difficulties, requires supplementing market wages. That this needs to be done I take to be beyond controversy: so long as we have human beings, some are going to fail for reason of ability, effort, or luck, and unless we're prepared to write them off we have to give them something. Especially given recent developments in the American labor market, moreover, we should be prepared to supplement their incomes far beyond what we've got in place today.

Of course, the possibility of getting something for nothing, or little, may distort incentives in inefficient or socially disruptive ways thereby creating, as with any redistributive scheme, "poverty trap" problems. If you give me enough when I don't work or when I have low take-home pay, I may forego a job or invest less in skills; or my employer may not give me a pay increase, since only a bit of it will show up in my after-tax-and-transfer income and it will have little effect on my performance. But the lion's share of these problems can be solved by work requirements at the employee's end and wage norming at the employer's.[8] The more substantive problem, in my view, is the general form of the wage supplement.

One way is to expand the "safety net" of supports for the very poor. Get some social agreement on the minimum acceptable income level, and when individuals fall below that fill in the gaps. At one time both conservatives and liberals supported a negative income tax. But this seemingly economically rational solution no longer commands much support anywhere.

Workers, be they poor or nonpoor, tend to be skeptical of programs that fund those who do not work. If the very poor have a serious physical or mental defect, we are willing to provide them with some funds, but if they are able-bodied, we are suspicious. Given this skepticism, means-tested programs for poor people risk becoming poor programs. Recently, this has produced the welfare "reform" that replaced "welfare as we know it" with "stingier welfare as we don't know it."

Another approach is to provide universal income supplements—some monetizable basket of goods or services provided to all citizens, irrespective of their labor market position—which I call a "social wage." Any expenditure on public goods—police protection, highways, public schools, parks, libraries—could count toward such a wage. So would national health insurance, or a universal citizen income grant. The important point is that a social wage is provided to all. This makes social wage programs politically popular since everyone gets, or expects or hopes to get, something from them. But it also can make them expensive, and socially inefficient in providing resources to some who just don't need them.

Is there a way to get the targeted efficiency of means-tested programs (making sure that the vast bulk of support goes to those who need the supplement) with the political appeal of universal ones? Or, asking the same question differently, is there a way to get a politically appealing "social wage" that doesn't bankrupt us all?

I think there is. We could treat social benefits the same as private incomes in the tax system, or perhaps even tax them more progressively.[9] Imagine a scheme in which social benefits were universal but in which the better-off who didn't really need them had the vast bulk taxed away. This is what President Reagan tried, in part, to do with his proposed taxation of the Social Security/medical benefits going to the wealthy elderly, but on which he was creamed by the AARP and Democrats and Republicans in the Congress. This is what President Clinton did by reducing the amount of Social Security that receives a tax break—leading Republicans to denounce him for "raising taxes" when they could just as easily have praised him for "reducing entitlements."

In the current U.S. political climate, I don't suppose this idea to be an easy one. But the logic for it is more or less impeccable, and we shouldn't plan forever on having a political debate in which reason never prevails. Properly configured, a "tax universalism" scheme with relatively low and flat rates of taxation on private income and steeply progressive taxation of social income could vastly improve the lot of the poor, and the middle class itself.

Consider the three stylized modes of redistribution: one approximating Europe's welfare state, the second approximating the United States, the third a social-wage welfare state. In all cases, the wealthy are assumed to earn much more than the middle class, while the poor have no incomes at all. In a European-style system, the wealthy and the middle class are subject to heavy taxation to pay for universal entitlements. In the U.S.-style scheme, lower rates of taxation underwrite a much-reduced basket of means-tested entitlements. In the social-wage solution, tax rates on private incomes would be progressive, though less steep than in Europe: a large basket of social benefits would be supplied to all, and those benefits would themselves be subject to steeply progressive taxes. The result has the potential to improve conditions not only for the poor but also for the middle class, which would benefit from the social wage and be allied with the poor by the workings of the social-wage system.

Whatever the precise details, there is a strong case for taxing income that comes in the form of social benefits at least as high as income that comes in the form of earnings. This is not a left/right issue. Taxing social-wage income even higher than private incomes may make sense to some, but not to others. However this issue is resolved, recentering the welfare state in this way is a way to institutionalize commitments to greater equality.

BUILD UNIONS

The natural private sector response to rising inequality and falling real earnings is for workers to form trade unions to bargain with employers over pay. To succeed, unions must win the support of a majority of workers at particular workplaces. But while U.S. law in theory permits workers to unionize through secret ballot elections and in theory encourages collective bargaining, the reality is that unionization is more difficult in our country than in any other advanced industrial society. It is, as Alison Porter of the AFL-CIO has described it, an act of courage for workers to try to unionize. They face a long election campaign in which supervisors may pressure them, and management threaten or fire them for their effort, with no guarantee of a collective bargaining contract at the end.

At the same time, U.S. labor law stifles other forms of employee workplace activity or organization for fear that they will become old-fashioned company unions. We have nothing like the works councils that nearly every European country mandates so that the company will hear employee voices. The result is that we are preventing the private sector from responding to inequality and falling real wages through the natural mechanism of collective action by workers.

This must change. Although the proportion of the U.S. workforce covered by unions has been falling for years, unions are still the single largest group of Americans concerned with, and committed to fighting, the new inequality. Indeed, without an enhanced union movement I cannot imagine how the United States can ever get itself organized to reduce the new inequality. The only measure adopted by the last Congress to combat inequality—the increase in the minimum wage—was passed through union pressure. The only effective way to increase the wages of low-wage and low-skill workers is through unionization. Survey after survey shows that low-paid workers—particularly low-paid African-American workers—want to join unions. Concentrated in the service sector, and thus largely safe from foreign competition, the lives of these workers could be substantially improved through the benefits of organization. If private sector unionization rose to 20 or 30 percent—and the polling data indicate that it would rise to that if workers had free choice—we would see a huge increase in pay and benefits at the bottom of the distribution.

However much or little you like unions, if you like the new inequality less you had better think of ways to strengthen the hand of your one sure ally.

New leadership at the AFL-CIO may herald a more successful union movement, so that labor will be able to resurrect by itself. But some form of labor law reform is probably needed to increase the ability of workers to exercise their right of association. Let me suggest one radical change: Let's get rid of federal preemption in labor law. Let the federal government set the minimum standards of protection, but let states vary, according to their wishes, above that. We already permit states to regulate public sector bargaining; but in the private sector, the gate only swings one way. States can ban union security clauses through so-called "right to work" amendments, but they aren't permitted to improve the conditions of worker organization. Why not let them do so?

What would result from this federal scheme? My guess is that the more heavily unionized states like New York, Minnesota, Illinois, and Hawaii would enact laws that made unionization easier; whereas states without significant union presence might want to further experiment with "labor management cooperation" schemes of the sort that present law at least on its face deters.[10] The result would be a jump in unionization in states that are favorable to unions; competition in the marketplace between those states and antiunion, right to work ones; and a proliferation of new forms of organizations. But the bottom line would be large increases in pay for service sector workers at the bottom of the earnings distribution in the unionizing areas, and a stronger movement to fight against the new inequality.

REBUILD CITIES

Anyone who has walked across Chicago's Midway, through the South Bronx, or a few blocks from the White House knows that we cannot conquer our inequality problem unless we so something about our cities. The most recent economic studies suggest even more: that cities are centers of hope as well as despair. By concentrating people, skill, and resources, they create "agglomeration" benefits—new ideas and production techniques generated through the interaction of their residents and communicated outward, externalities from environmental improvement—that spur economic growth.

What might we do to make something of this potential? For all their good intent, Jack Kemp's empowerment zones are not the way to go for a simple reason: they are not cost-effective. They are simply another form of ineffective trickle-down. Many of our current urban and transportation programs might usefully be eliminated immediately, since all they do is pave the way for employers to leave cities. We would take a big step forward to end programs that subsidize the destruction of our cities. But we can do more: invest in the physical and social infrastructure—from effective mass transit systems to functioning schools to public safety, sectoral training consortia, modernization services—that will enhance cities and that may more than pay for themselves as they provide a base for thriving urban businesses that rely upon an abundant supply of high-quality public goods, of the sort that cities, given their population densities, are best able to afford.

Resuscitating cities will require some reduction of regulatory red tape and elimination of municipal corruption and featherbedding. It will be enhanced by local adoption of metropolitan forms of governance and taxation. We've made it too easy to avoid the burdens of city life without sacrificing the benefits by moving a few miles out. Rebuilding our metro regions could be accompanied by institutionalizing regional government.

Last, at their core—and immediately—we need to make the poor areas of cities more passably livable. One need not be a conservative to see the logic of better police

protection nor an old liberal to see the logic of better social services for the inner-city poor, not simply to resurrect the cities but to provide the social wage that all citizens merit. We cannot isolate "them" in city slums while
"we" live in protected suburban areas. If we do, we will
have lost the war against the new inequality and created
my nightmare apartheid economy

How to Think about This

These five strategies require substantial reordering of
policy priorities. They face any number of locked-in interest groups resisting their advance; and they may give
offense to all ideological camps, your own among them.
But they have the advantage of sidestepping received categories of debate and partisan policies. We are all tired of
the old political debates between the liberals (wherever
they are) and conservatives, do-littles and do-nothings,
Donkeys and Elephants. We have a real problem that
must be solved, and ideology should not constrain our
design of policies to solve it.

The unifying theme of the five strategies is to achieve
equal opportunity by leveling the playing field. We ensure people the resources they need to compete in the
market on fair terms through asset redistribution,
starting-gate intervention, and a social safety net of universal but taxed benefits. We ensure that those who are
better off don't exploit their advantages by easing the

conditions of organization for workers. And we concentrate resources on cities, where concentrations of poverty are greatest and social investments most likely to pay off.

If you are conservative, note that all these strategies are respectful of what markets can do efficiently, of property rights (wanting to enlarge in the case of workers!), and the need for productivity and contribution; they simply widen the range of people able to make that contribution, and don't rely on impoverishment as a spur to its being made. If you are a liberal, note that all these strategies seek to achieve your desired ends—relief of poverty, an expanded middle class—though not through the government-led administration of people you have traditionally favored. If you are a progressive, note that strategies along these lines seem like decent bets, and ones that distinguish your commitments from the sham policies currently making the rounds.

But whatever you are, and whether you find these five strategies attractive or not, I hope you agree that we must find a cure to the inequality problem that is gnawing, like a cancer, at the soul of our country—and that you agree that the way to do this is to be open to plans regardless of their ideological or political pedigree. If you reject my proposals, don't attack me, or my ideas, or even my profession: attack the problem. Let's find what looks most promising, and then organize and fight for those plans. Give 'em hell—or whatever—with something new.

II

Through a Gendered Lens

HEIDI HARTMANN

*R*ichard Freeman's analysis of why we should be concerned about growing inequality in the United States and his suggestions for what we can do about it are good starting points for discussion, but looking at the same issues through a gendered lens provides a different understanding of the same phenomena and several alternative policy directions to explore.

For example: In discussing the growing inequality in earnings, Freeman stresses declining real wages for the majority of men, especially men at the bottom, since the mid-1970s. He mentions in passing that women were the only low-earning group who saw their real wages rise. (Actually, women's wages have fallen at the very bottom, too, but for most women they rose, and thus they rose on average.) During the 1980s, the wage gap between women and men closed by about 10 percentage points—from a gap of 40 percent at a ratio of 0.60 (women's earnings to men's) to a gap of 30 percent at the current earnings ratio of 0.70. The gap closed both because men's real wages fell and because women's real wages increased.

While earnings inequality was increasing among both women and men (though more among men), the addition of women's earnings to family income helped to equalize the income distribution among families. Thus an important, though unmentioned, way to reduce inequality among families in the United States would be to continue to bring women's wages up to men's. Not only would achieving pay equity increase fairness for individuals—perhaps increasing their faith in the markets Freeman reveres—it would also serve to reduce poverty significantly, especially the poverty of our poorest families: those headed by women alone. Such families now account for 24 percent of all families with minor children and 60 percent of all poor families with children. The set of policies Freeman proposes, though worthy of further exploration, would do little to address the specific needs of these families. The social welfare policies of the European states, which Freeman seems ambivalent about (on the one hand he disparages their social insurance, tax-transfer base; on the other he lauds their tendency to shift resources toward the early years) do address these needs. More on this point below.

Let's consider why women's earnings rose. In doing so, we can see both the advantages and the limits of one of Freeman's proposed strategies, equalizing human capital accumulation through educational opportunities. At least partly as a result of federal legislation such as Title

IX, women are closing the educational gap between themselves and men; more women than men are now graduating from college and earning masters' degrees. And there's no question that their more rapid accumulation of human capital contributed to the narrowing of the wage gap noted above. Yet women's earnings, at 70 percent of men's on average, still lag far behind. Without effective antidiscrimination measures in the labor market to monitor how the race is run, the starting-gate equality Freeman stresses won't lead to the results we want.

More generally, Freeman's endorsement of the marketplace as the sorting and rewarding mechanism for us all must give those of us who fare less well in the market substantial reason for concern. While Freeman may be right that the ascendancy of free-enterprise conservatives in U.S. political life behooves all of us to look for the equality-enhancing opportunities in market-oriented policies, I hope that at least some progressive economists (and others) will train their sights on market failure and the ways in which we must regulate markets to help them come closer to achieving their theoretical efficiencies. If, as has been said, markets come out of the barrel of a gun, then it would be difficult to isolate markets and market outcomes from the underlying distribution of power.

The only challenge to the present distribution of market power endorsed by Freeman is the union movement.

A good choice, but not sufficient (though it is true that now that unions have become more inclusive in their membership, they help women and minority men as much as, if not more than, their traditional membership of white men). A strong government and rational, reasonable regulations are needed to control the worst excesses of capital and of markets run amok. And income transfers, taxes, and government programs are needed when markets can't or won't work.

Transfers deal with a fundamental problem of market capitalism: some people don't have enough dollar votes to buy what they need to survive, and especially not to survive at a level beneficial to society as a whole. (I'm not sure why Freeman thinks there will be less resistance to assets transfers than income transfers, and I note he proposes to fund the transition with taxes.)

Taxes and government programs are necessary when the operation of markets won't result in a socially optimum outcome, the classic example being defense. As Jesse Jackson was fond of asking during his presidential campaigns: How many of you have cruise missiles in your backyard? (No hands up.) Now, how many of you have VCRs in your homes? (Lots of hands.) Jesse was actually illustrating something else (that the U.S. produces what no one wants, while Japan produces what everyone wants) but his point applies here as well: if you buy a missile it will also protect me, and I won't have to pay; but if nobody buys one then we won't have enough defense. There's some evidence to suggest that, on average, parents don't buy enough goods and services for their children even when they have enough dollar votes. (And since we expect less and less that children will take care of us when we are infirm, why is such spending rational anyway?) So societies use taxes to transfer resources from adults to children, in support of public education, for example. In the United States, the share of income taxes paid by corporations has fallen, while that paid by individuals and families has increased. Perhaps corporations can pick up more of the tab for children.

A much greater investment in children—free, universally available child care, more health care, and income support when needed—is warranted, then, for many reasons. Paid family leave for working parents is another way to shift resources to the benefit of the young. A recent study by the Institute for Women's Policy Research shows that a program providing up to 12 weeks of paid leave (for the same reasons that many workers are now entitled to unpaid leave under the 1993 Family and Medical Leave Act), if all employers were required to participate, would cost about the same as our current unemployment insurance system. Programs such as these would help all families with children but would do most for the poorest and for single parents who lack a spouse for backup child-care or income support.

Many social insurance programs work well. Medicare and Medicaid, for example, have very low administrative costs compared to private health insurance plans. Let's look twice before we abandon tried and true income-based vehicles for the asset-based schemes of academic economists.

I fear that Richard Freeman's "ideal virgin capitalism" will somehow wind up screwing us all.

What Consensus?

PAUL R. KRUGMAN

I don't want to seem to quibble with Richard Freeman's essay, since I am overwhelmingly in agreement with it. Let me just make a few points.

First, I think Freeman is overly optimistic when he asserts that there is consensus on the fact of drastically increased inequality. It is true that all reasonable people are now agreed on this fact, but unreasonable people have a lot of influence in this country. Recently the *National Review* ran an article asserting, yet again, that the only evidence for growing inequality comes from fraudulent statistics concocted by liberals, while the St. Louis Fed published yet another spurious study claiming that hardly anybody stays in the bottom quintile for more than a few years. The persistence of such views mainly reflects the ability of some wealthy people to buy "research" that caters to their prejudices and interests, but it means that getting a consensus on action is going to be even harder than Freeman thinks.

Second, the debate over causes is a bit more important than Freeman suggests, because there is a significant bloc of opinion that thinks that closing off international trade is the answer to the problem of inequality. We can and should argue that protectionism is a bad idea because of its side consequences—not least for workers in developing countries—but it is also important to realize that it simply would not work, because most of the rise in inequality is explained by other causes.

Anyway, on to Freeman's five strategies. I want to comment mainly on the first (asset-based redistribution) and fourth (build unions). I agree entirely with the rest.

I like Freeman's idea of providing each individual with a trust fund when young rather than retirement benefits when old, but we had better realize that this is a significant change in the character of the social insurance system. Social Security is structured from the point of view of the recipients as if it were an ordinary retirement plan: what you get out depends on what you put in. So it does not look like a redistributionist scheme. In practice it has turned out to be strongly redistributionist, but only because of its Ponzi game aspect, in which each generation takes more out than it put in. Well, the Ponzi game will soon be over, thanks to changing demographics, so that the typical recipient henceforth will get only about as much as he or she put in (and today's young may well get less than they put in).

Freeman's scheme, however, will necessarily be frankly redistributionist, because the trust fund you receive when young cannot be based on what you will actually pay into the system over the rest of your life. Presumably the size of the trust fund will be the same for everyone—which means that some people will receive much more than the present value of the trust-fund taxes they pay over the rest of their lives, others much less. Now I don't have any problem with that kind of redistribution, but I think we had better realize that it will face intense opposition, that its "capitalistic" aspects will probably not buy off many of the critics.

Put it this way: Freeman may think that it is a shared value that everyone should have an equal chance at the start of life; but it isn't. On the contrary, recent news reports tell us that the next big push by tax-cutters will be a drive to eliminate the inheritance tax—that is, what the right wants more than anything else is to allow the wealthy to pass on their status to their children.

On a related point: I could not figure out from this essay what Freeman thinks of the Earned Income Tax Credit, which is also a frankly redistributionist scheme, but whose link to willingness to work has given it at least a fragile political acceptance. Isn't a significant expansion (say a tripling) of the EITC program the line of least resistance way to do something about incomes at the bottom?

On to union-building. I agree totally with Freeman here: even if you don't like unions very much, even if you think they often reduce efficiency, we need them as a social and political counterweight to the power of wealth in our country. What I would say is that this is a much broader point than just unions. The stunning fact about U.S. political economy over the past 25 years is that policy has reinforced rather than opposed the growth in inequality—a fact best explained by observing that the growing concentration of wealth has also led to a growing concentration of power in the hands of the wealthy. What this means is that if you are serious about pursuing the goal of limiting inequality you must think strategically; you should ask about any proposed policy change not only how it directly affects less well-off Americans, but also how it will affect the future political balance. For example, proposals for school vouchers should be critiqued not only on educational or cost-efficiency grounds but also because they raise the risk of a collapse in the political support for public education. (If upper-middle-class families are allowed to "top up" their vouchers with their own money, they will soon realize that it is in their interest to cut the size of the vouchers as much as possible). And—dare we say it?—we should in general oppose privatization plans if they are likely to destroy public sector unions. After all, people on the right tend to favor privatization for exactly the same reason.

I have to admit that I am fairly cynical about the prospects for the kind of bipartisan, cut-across-the-political-divide assault on inequality that Freeman hopes for. Right now we have a powerful conservative movement that cannot really bring itself to admit the fact of inequality, let alone talk about solutions; and right-wingers are furious and embittered by the outrageous willingness of their middle-of-the-road opponents to play political hardball as fiercely as they do. At the moment it is hard to imagine much more than a modest expansion of the EITC. But we do need a discussion of how to make a broader assault on inequality, to prepare the ground for the time when some real action may be possible.

Promoting the Common Good

MICHAEL PIORE

I share Richard Freeman's concern about increasing income inequality in the United States and declining welfare for people at the lower end of the distribution. I also share his frustration at the indifference of the electorate and much of the political and policy-making community. And I admire his inventiveness in proposing new strategies to overcome the current impasse. But I am considerably less enthusiastic about the strategies themselves.

This is in part because I do not see the current tendencies in the distribution of income as indicative of social trends more broadly. Indeed, while I would give much more weight than Freeman apparently does to the deliberate policies of the Reagan—and, to a lesser extent, Bush and Clinton—administrations in producing an increasing dispersion of income, I think we should also recognize the progress made on other fronts in reducing economic disadvantage and social stigma. In the last 15 years, that progress has been particularly marked for women, the physically handicapped, gays and lesbians, and Asian-Americans. Much of this progress has not been economic in the narrow sense of the term but it has greatly changed the lived experience of the members of these groups in American society. Also noteworthy: in possibly the most conservative period in American politics, we have managed to preserve the gains made in the late 1960s and 1970s in the economic welfare and social status of African-Americans and the aged. With the possible exception of the aged, I do not see comparable gains for disadvantaged and socially stigmatized groups in other advanced industrial societies—despite their much more even distribution of income.

It may not be completely clear why this particular pattern of social redress has emerged, but a very important factor must be the growing self-consciousness of these groups and their increasing political awareness and cohesion. This contrasts strongly with the declining strength and cohesion of work as a source of identity and locus of political organization, and of the labor movement as a political and economic force. This does not translate directly into the declining income at the bottom of the distribution. Neither low income nor the jobs with which it is associated have ever been a source of identity or effective political organization. One of the enduring characteristics of low-income individuals not identified closely with racial and ethnic communities in the United States is their social and political isolation (a point to which I will return below). But among identity groups effective in the political process, the labor move-

ment is the one for which a reduction in income disparities is most critical to its broader mission. There is thus
much ground for optimism in the fact that the decline in
union strength seems to have leveled off, and that the
AFL-CIO has finally begun a process of organizational
renewal with new leadership and aggressive campaigns
to organize new members and reassert itself in the political process. The welfare of low-income workers is an in-
tegral part of these campaigns. Because part of labor's
problem is that it had come to be associated in the public
mind with the privileged position of its own members,
the prominence which the revived union movement is
giving to low-income work is likely to have a dual effect.
As it increases public awareness and concern for those at
the bottom of the labor market, it will change the public
perception of the labor movement.

The recent history of the labor movement carries an
important lesson for American social movements more
generally. Such movements can gain broad public support for remedial policies, even policies which seem to
compromise other core American values: that is what the
labor movement did through legislation and court rul-
ings curtailing employer free speech and private property rights; that is what women and racial minorities did
through affirmative action. But such public support is
contingent on the credibility of the claims which the
groups make to promote the general welfare, and not
only their own particular interests. When movements

seem to retreat from these broader claims, when they come to be perceived as exclusively dedicated to the pursuit of particularistic concerns of their immediate constituencies, the public becomes intolerant of special policies which protect them. The incipient reaction against affirmative action suggests that the black movement and women's movement are coming to be perceived in the way that labor was in the 1970s. To avoid a similar fate they will have to move quickly, as the labor movement has somewhat belatedly, to reemphasize the problems of their low-income brothers and sisters who have not benefited so clearly from the success of the group as a whole.

This brings us to the question of what kinds of policies it makes sense for movements dedicated to social progress to advocate in the political arena. Of Freeman's five strategies only the proposal to strengthen unions seems both to lend itself to this kind of advocacy and to have real promise for reversing trends in income inequality. But given the need of organized labor to overcome the perception that it is a "narrow," "special" interest, it would be a mistake for it to use its re-emergent political power to demand new protective legislation. What is required, it seems to me, is a much more focused policy than Freeman proposes. In particular, I would propose a two part policy: the first part would seek to raise the minimum wage over the next ten years at a rate substantially in excess of average wage increases (say two times the average). The second part would be a concerted effort to enforce the full range of labor legislation regulating low wage employment: minimum wage laws, equal employment opportunity legislation, sanctions on employers hiring undocumented aliens, unemployment insurance and social security taxes, health and safety legislation, as well as the right to organize and bargain collectively.

I would place particular emphasis on equal employment opportunity and employer sanctions. One of the factors depressing wages at the bottom of the labor market over the last two decades has been the progressive substitution of immigrant labor for American nationals, particularly African-Americans. This occurred, especially in the beginning, because American nationals did not want menial, low-wage jobs. But it has also happened because the availability of immigrant workers has combined with the deterioration of labor standards and their increasingly lax enforcement to make it unnecessary for employers to improve job offers to attract labor. Meanwhile, equal employment opportunity enforcement ignored this sector of the labor market to focus on more attractive job opportunities. And the Labor Department's Wages and Hours Division, which enforces minimum wage legislation, shifted resources from that task to enforcing laws governing equal pay for women and minorities, again at the high end of the market. The enforcement of employer sanctions should be accomplished by shifting resources from apprehending workers to apprehending employers who hire them. When jobs are no longer available, the flow of foreign labor to the United States should diminish sufficiently to alleviate downward pressure on wages. Those who remain, or continue to come, will tend to have family ties and relations of the kind which will eventually lead to a regularization of their legal status. We need not demonize or criminalize foreign nationals simply for wanting to raise their income by taking jobs in the United States. But we also need to recognize that job opportunities in the United States are rationed, at least at the bottom of the labor market. The twin instruments of equal employment opportunity and employer sanctions enforce rationing criteria consistent with public policy; in their absence, employers pick a set of criteria dictated by private economic interests and prejudices that, experience shows, are destructive of internal equity and undermine social stability.

Freeman's proposal to delegate legislation protecting and regulating the right to organize and bargain collectively is intriguing. In some ways, it simply implements the logic of NAFTA, or, more broadly, the globalization of economic activity. If we live and work in a world where U.S. workers already compete directly with the radically different labor law regimes of Canada and Mexico, why should we be particularly concerned with uniformity within our own borders? The states already control the legal regimes governing collective bargaining by state and local employees, and this has become an increasingly large component of collective bargaining activity. On the other hand, this strategy seems inconsistent: If we are concerned with income inequality, how can we be indifferent to the inequality of bargaining power that produces it? If competition among countries has failed to reduce income inequality (indeed, is one of the leading candidates to explain its current increase) why should competition among states have a different result? The more consistent proposal would be to impose the logic of uniformity upon the process of globalization. I would, in fact, as soon adopt the labor legislation of any one of our neighbors as I would delegate it to the states. Mexican labor legislation—or that of virtually any of the Canadian provinces—would do more to strengthen unions in the United States than the legislation which even the most progressive states here would be likely to pass under Freeman's proposal.

I also have problems with Freeman's other proposals. Freeman expresses an interest, for example, in urban economic development, but offers no concrete proposals. Though the agglomeration effects upon which he would build an urban policy have recently attracted interest from economists, they are not new. The way they have been played out in recent years mirrors the growing disparity in the rest of the economy. On the one side are high-income agglomerations built around high-tech industries and finance from which the poor are excluded by their educational background. On the other side are low-wage agglomerations in such industries as garments, which have been a traditional path for upward social mobility. The latter opportunities have been severely restricted by globalization, but they remain and have become a channel for advancement for new immigrant groups. The fact that urban garment centers in the United States have managed to survive at all attests to the substantial locational advantages of agglomeration and market proximity: these industries quite probably would sustain much higher wages than they now pay. But as in other low-wage industries, their wages have been declining in recent years and the American-born poor, particularly African-Americans, are—again, originally by their own choice but now by employer policy—increasingly excluded. The first task is thus not to create new agglomerations but to raise wages and open up jobs in those that are already there.

The more serious problem an urban strategy needs to address is social isolation. The isolation of the urban poor is probably the major impediment to their organizing on their own behalf. It has been increased by central-city violence, which has led people to withdraw further into their own homes. We need to experiment less with enterprise zones than with urban safety zones where airport-like security and police saturation might create secure public spaces in which people could associate with each other.

My strongest objection, however, is to addressing poverty through capital endowments. The management of financial risk in a capitalist society requires considerable expertise. Even to purchase such expertise on the market requires a good deal more knowledge about finance than most people in our society now have. I imagine that we could achieve a broader distribution of the requisite competence. But I do not see how we could develop it widely enough to protect the endowments initially created to solve the income distribution problem. And if we did, the result would be a civilization completely obsessed with financial management. Though I would be hard pressed to choose between that civilization and one which tolerates the income disparities we seem now to be developing, I do not believe that we face that depressing choice.

New Ideas?

FRANCES FOX PIVEN

I'm sure everyone in this conversation agrees that the growth of unions and the revival of our older cities make sense as steps to reverse sharply increasing inequalities. These are not new solutions, of course, but old solutions whose importance has been underlined as the effects of union decline and urban decay have accumulated. However, I am taken aback by what is new here, namely Freeman's proposal to devolve authority over labor law from the federal government to the states. The states have generally been even more business-oriented than the national government, in large part because they are susceptible to the threats or enticements of business relocation. To make labor protections subject to the ongoing bidding wars that corporations initiate between the states is a recipe for labor helplessness.

Freeman's big idea for egalitarian reform is to shift from income redistribution to asset redistribution. This is indeed newer. But even proposals for asset redistribution have precedents that deserve scrutiny for the lessons they suggest. The idea of turning worker pension funds into a capital instrument for social ends has been around for a while. It flared and fizzled because it never seemed to capture the imagination of workers, perhaps because they were not stirred by the prospect of risking their pensions for socially desirable investment. And older ESOP schemes also evoked the promise of redistributing wealth and power, but in practice did little of either, as visions of worker power turned into mere paper ownership of firms controlled by managers and markets. The point here, I think, is generalizable: schemes for asset redistribution are inevitably swamped by the market forces they are intended to temper, so that the egalitarian terms of "virgin capitalism" have to be continually reconstructed. This is no small feat.

Asset redistribution, dependent on sharply increased inheritance and income taxes, will generate enormous opposition, and especially if it goes beyond paper rights (as the Swedish unions learned with the failure of the Meidner plan). Freeman doesn't want to talk about political feasibility. But if the game is to talk about what would be nice to have, then why not also talk about a big wealth tax that would move toward reversing asset concentration, and even provide the resources that might make possible a viable public sector?

That said, I want to agree with the argument that workers are likely to be better corporate decision-makers, simply because worker interests are multifaceted, going beyond a singular preoccupation with the bottom line and the short-term to include concerns with, for example, job security and community well-being. This is the old promise in proposals for worker owner-ship, and it remains compelling to me.

I am even more uneasy about Freeman's related pro-posals for reform of the welfare state. True, many of our current programs are badly flawed; support levels and coverage are typically inadequate, especially for the poor and unemployed, and the terms of aid can be humiliat-ing. But I doubt that Freeman's approach will help. In fact, I worry that his call for shifting funds from the aged to the young is dangerous. It contributes to widespread efforts already afoot to discredit Social Security and Medicare. These are arguably the most popular and suc-cessful programs of the American welfare state. They have accomplished a historic reduction in old age pov-erty, and increased the security of working people who otherwise supported aged relatives and also faced the prospect of their own penury in old age. Now the pro-grams are taking a terrific propaganda battering from the right, the left, and the middle.

One argument, which Freeman seems to accept, is that programs for the aged are eating up the funds that could otherwise be spent on the young and the poor. This assumes that all other important items of the bud-get are fixed, including expenditures on the military and corporate welfare, and the tax givebacks of the past two decades. And even if we accepted this assumption for the purpose of argument, what sensible political reason is there to think that funds taken from Social Security and Medicare would somehow, miraculously, come to be allocated to programs for the poor and the young? After all, it is these latter programs that have proved so politically vulnerable in the past two decades. Freeman wants to talk about solutions "regardless of their pedigree or feasibility." But policy proposals are obviously an aspect of political strategy. Does it make sense to begin the difficult struggle to reduce inequality in America by considering solutions which tear away at the sources of popular support for past successes?

Running through these proposals is the idea that market-conforming reforms are more viable than reforms which depend on a vigorous public sector. Thus, shifting funds from the aged to the young will contribute to economic productivity. Parts of the social wage should be made conditional on work. Asset redistribution might increase savings. But the bearing of increased economic productivity on income and wealth inequalities is by no means clear. As Freeman points out, the proportion of the population in paid employment in the United States has grown in tandem with spiraling inequalities. And this approach to reform misses or dismisses what is I think the main achievement of liberal welfare state programs, which is that they reduce inequality partly by creating a politically determined income floor which enhances worker security, and therefore worker bargaining power.

In sum, I don't think worsening inequality is the result of tired old ideas about programs. I think it is more the result of the growing power of business, and the correlative demoralization and confusion of democratic opposition. True, ideas have something to do with power, if only because they legitimate its exercise and reveal its promise. But the big ideas at work here don't seem to me to be very new. The idea of the unfettered market that legitimates rising business power is not a new idea. And the best idea to justify resistance to that power, the idea of a democratic state with the authority and resources to tame predatory market actors, is not new either.

A Liberal Agenda

JAMES TOBIN

Richard Freeman is certainly right that unprecedented inequality of wealth, income, and wages in
America is a crisis threatening the sense of community,
the essential foundation of the republic. As he says, the
crisis deserves urgent attention. Economists and other
social scientists need to seek possible remedies. Alas,
effective policies are very hard to find. I shall discuss in
turn the five planks in Freeman's own platform.

Asset-based redistributions. America likes to describe itself as the land of equal opportunity. Conservatives in
particular emphasize this equality to differentiate it from
equality of outcomes and conditions. They choose to ignore the unpleasant reality that one generation's inequality of outcomes is the next generation's inequality of
opportunity.

Freeman would like to soften this connection by some
redistribution of assets. This requires, it seems to me,
progressive taxation of estates and intergenerational
gifts, and of income. A logical but radical instrument
would be a progressive wealth tax. Private net wealth in
the United States is about $25 trillion, 3.5 times GDP.

The most important asset we should help the young to

acquire is human capital. We should emphasize education from preschool to post–high school, with national standards and federal financial help. We should promote health from womb through adolescence. We should provide needs-tested financial aid for education after high school, offering grants and loans with repayments dependent on subsequent incomes. In the past I have proposed in the *New Republic* universal "youth endowments," an idea suggested by the successes of the G.I. Bill; these too could require income-conditioned repayments. In motivation, this proposal was like Freeman's asset redistribution.

In today's conservative politics, these all look like nonstarters, unless the national mood can be changed by appreciation of the perils of the status quo. Anyway, they are preferable to the currently fashionable tax credits or deductions, which mainly are windfalls for the middle- and upper-bracket students who would be going to school beyond 12th grade anyway.

I sympathize with Freeman's proposal to give worker owners control of their own pension funds. I would also like to see each individual worker's pension claims vested and portable. But these reforms will do little to redistribute assets to workers at the bottom, whose jobs rarely offer pension plans anyway.

Beware of privatization of Social Security. I am afraid it will have regressive distributional effects. It is unlikely to open any doors Freeman would want to pass through.

Starting-gate equality. Some of my remarks above apply here as well. I don't find anything in particular wrong about the degree of redistribution we now have between affluent elderly and poor elderly. Indeed we could do more of this, without destroying the elements of universal insurance in Social Security and Medicare. Affluent elderly should pay much more than they do now for Medicare Part B, which is not covered by the hospital insurance trust fund but is heavily subsidized from general revenues. The most affluent should pay the entire cost of nonhospital health care insurance.

In the spirit of Freeman's preference for redistribution at earlier ages, I have proposed that the government "pay" the payroll taxes of workers with abnormally low earnings in any year.

Social wages and targeting benefits. I suppose that treating social benefits as taxable income—including in-kind benefits and values of public goods only to the extent they are taxable to other people as well—is psychologically and politically helpful, even if it is substantively meaningless. As an old proponent of the "negative income tax," I believe that we should give the poor positive incentives to earn income and to live in families, even if this means that some nonpoor households will be receiving a bit of cash. If the incentives of moderate marginal tax rates are good for the rich, why are they not good for the poor? The Earned Income Tax Credit is a step in the right direction. It should be strengthened.

Build unions. I don't see this proposal as necessarily improving the distribution of wage incomes. It might raise wages for organized workers with skills and bargaining power relative to, perhaps even at the expense of, less fortunate workers. It might increase labor incomes at the expense of capital incomes in some sectors. But past experience cannot make me optimistic that it will change the aggregate shares of labor and capital in GDP significantly. There may, however, be other reasons for rectifying the balance of power between employers and workers.

Rebuild cities. Amen! I think we should implement the proposals of Bill Wilson: government as employer of last resort, hiring the residents of inner cities to rebuild their own districts. Tax credits for private employers will never do the job. Harry Hopkins's WPA is the right model. This does not exclude government-financed big projects, constructing and renovating houses, schools, clinics, streets, and other capital facilities of civilization.

Remarks. Let specific proposals stand on their substantive merits. There's no need to label them ideologically. Yet neither should we deceive ourselves. If "liberal" means anything in current politics it describes a willingness to use the public fisc to make economic well-being less unequal than market earnings. If "conservative" means anything today, it means that unequal market earnings should prevail, scarcely modified by taxes and transfers. Freeman's proposals for redistribution are liberal.

Old Problem, New Despair

JAMES HECKMAN

*R*ichard Freeman accurately describes the recent rise in wage and income inequality in the United States. He speculates about its consequences, and proposes five policies to alleviate it.

Wages were no more unequally distributed in 1990 than in 1940. They were even more unequally distributed during the Depression and in earlier periods of economic stress. Our democratic society was preserved then, albeit with strain. Democracy and the social order can survive at higher levels of earnings inequality than those experienced in the 1960s.

What is different now is the trend. After 1940, inequality was substantially reduced. The reduction came because the real wages of the least skilled increased more rapidly than the real wages of the skilled, although both grew substantially in the postwar period. A whole generation became accustomed to this trend which started early in this century. One could make a good living even if one dropped out of school.

What fuels the post-1980 rise in wage inequality is the absolute decline in real wages for the unskilled caused by a shift in demand away from them. Until recently, such a decline only occurred during depressions or severe crises when wages of all workers decreased. Now, however, the wages of the unskilled are declining when the wages of the skilled are rising. However, in the past two years the data indicate that this trend has halted. Expectations about success in the labor market were dramatically changed for a whole generation of unskilled workers. Standard measures of earnings inequality understate the severity of the problem because they exclude nonearners, and ignore the decline of fringe benefits among the least skilled. Among that group, nonemployment and lack of any earnings has substantially increased.

When Freeman and others write about the problem of inequality, they are concerned about this phenomenon, not inequality per se, although some of Freeman's proposals seem directed toward solving the problem of inequality and not the problem of declining real wages. The principal issue is to raise living standards at the bottom. Redistributive policies aimed at eliminating inequality miss the point. Our current problem is not that some are doing better than others, but rather the despair among the least skilled, who have become detached from the modern economy. If the trend continues, it will promote participation in the social pathologies of crime, welfare, and illegitimacy. Even if the trend has stabilized, the level of wages is still low for the least skilled.

In addressing the problem of the unskilled, it is important to take a long view while at the same time recognizing the problems of social dislocation caused by the new labor market. In general terms, Freeman is right when he speculates that the most effective long-run policy is to target interventions early in life. More specifically, all the available evidence points to the great long-run value of raising the skill levels and motivation of the very young. Research in psychology and economics indicates that skill begets skill; early learning promotes later learning. Investment in the education and training of the very young earns a far higher return than investment placed in a teenager or middle-age adult. John Donohue of Stanford Law School and Peter Siegelman of Yale Law School have estimated that the benefits of reduced crime alone more than pay for the costs of an enriched Head Start program targeted toward disadvantaged youth.[1]

With older workers, matters are more complicated. Policies that improve skills can help, but my research and that of others demonstrates that such policies are very costly, even if applied to unskilled and low-ability youth in their late teens, and certainly if applied to older workers. The economic return to education and training for these people is so low that a more useful policy would be to subsidize their employment. Job subsidies offer an attractive alternative to welfare: they promote employment, integrate the unskilled into the economy, and provide them, their communities, and their children with the dignity and social benefit of work. I have developed this argument elsewhere.[2]

Subsidies can take many forms. The Earned Income Tax Credit is one program that creates financial incentives for low-income persons to work. Other subsidy programs would induce employers to hire low-skill workers at high wages by compensating them for the gap between wages and productivity of their unskilled workers. Targeting job subsidies too narrowly and at too low a benefit level can backfire, however, and it is important to avoid stigmatization. If subsidies are given only to very low-skill workers with severe motivation problems, and the subsidy is not sufficiently large, research by Gary Burtless of Brookings reveals that employers view the subsidy as a warning label and do not hire subsidized workers.

In contrast, policies that reduce the demand for the unskilled, like minimum wage laws or increases in union wage scales, are generally bad ideas. They increase the wages of those who remain employed but at the same time have the perverse effect of increasing inequality among the least skilled, and reducing their employment.

What about Organizing?

ERNESTO CORTES, JR.

*F*irst of all, let me congratulate Richard Freeman on his cogent analysis of the crisis facing our nation, and state my belief that Freeman's thesis is correct: The decline in the average wages of 80 percent of working families and resulting increase in inequality threatens the very foundation of American civil society. Which brings us back to what Freeman correctly identifies as the most fundamental question, "What do we do about it?"

But before we deal with that question, I believe we have to try to understand why there is no outcry about the increase in inequality. The leaders and organizers of the Industrial Areas Foundation (IAF) have been studying the decline in real wages and the increases in inequality for nearly a decade. We know the statistics are true. So why is there no national debate?

I have come to the conclusion that at least three factors are at work. First, the devastating changes in the economy, of which Freeman so eloquently writes, have occurred relatively slowly over the last two decades. Second, the increases in economic inequality reinforce themselves. By this I mean that as the gap between working families and the politicians and their wealthy patrons continues to increase, the decision-makers become less capable of understanding or even developing an awareness of those most impacted by the economic devastation.

Third, and perhaps most importantly, the institutions that would have once brought these families into relationship with one another and developed their capacities to articulate an effective public position reflecting their common interests and concerns have all but disappeared in most communities. The community-based institutions which once would have served as the vehicles for public outcry about declining wages—the congregations, the Settlement Homes, the workers' associations —these institutions have unraveled to the point where they are at best service centers organized to deal with the consequences of declining incomes.

By and large, the research conducted by the leaders of the IAF supports Richard Freeman's conclusions about the inadequacies of the strategies currently being pursued by elected officials. However, we have a small disagreement with his assertion that increased government training programs "cannot make more than a small dent toward reversing the rise of inequality." While it is quite correct that a three- or even six-month training program will not restore a 20 percent downward trend in real earnings, our experiences with long-term job training programs indicate that 18 months to two years of training for mid- to high-skilled positions currently available in the local labor market can go a long way toward improving the economic situation of participants. MIT professor Paul Osterman's study of Project QUEST in San Antonio concludes that not only did participants make considerable economic gains relative to their prior wage and income levels, but that Project QUEST participants increased their wages at a higher rate than the average increase for all employees in Bexar County. Other significant positive outcomes include the opportunity for further education and training through employers, as well as such benefits as health insurance and retirement funds.

In organizing communities around the well-being of families throughout the United States, IAF leaders have reached a number of conclusions that reinforce the proposals outlined in Freeman's five strategies for "raising the bottom and reducing inequality." In particular we believe that redistributing resources to support individuals earlier in their lives is critical to sustaining a civil society in this nation. Our organizations have found that resources invested in public education, after-school programs, preventive health care for children, summer work experiences for adolescents, college scholarships, and similar strategies greatly improve the chances of those children when they become adults. Decades of experience have allowed our organizations to see the adults these children become. These children have become leaders in their community and the leaders of our organizations.

The Alliance Schools Initiative is a relatively recent strategy developed by the leaders of the IAF. As described by professors Frank Levy and Richard Murnane in *Teaching the New Basic Skills*, this initiative is a strategy for increasing student achievement through the kind of school restructuring that can only be created and sustained through the work of a broad-based collective constituency of parents, teachers, administrators, and community leaders. Not only has student achievement increased relative to previous achievement at these schools, but as Levy and Murnane outline in the September 11, 1996, edition of *Education Week*, the Alliance Schools in Austin increased student achievement and attendance relative to schools of similar socioeconomic status which received equal amounts of supplemental resources.

While it may be too broad, our interpretation of this information is that resource transfers—particularly in terms of education—will improve the health of the nation only to the extent that an organized constituency is prepared to operate differently with those extra resources. To put it bluntly, increased resources are necessary, but not sufficient to "raise the bottom and reduce inequality." And I suspect this will hold true for all five of Freeman's proposed strategies.

Which brings me to our only serious concern about Freeman's very thoughtful and eloquent article. In the text, I noted only a very few references to what the IAF believes is the most important strategy of all—the organizing of a broad-based constituency for change. And as our experience has taught us, it is the strategy on which the success of all the other strategies depend. Yet organizing is the strategy that most progressives talk about least.

Imagine what would happen if, in 75 congressional districts, each candidate attended a meeting with 2,500 to 3,000 organized, registered voters—each of whom was committed to turning out at least ten of their neighbors on election day. What if at those public meetings each candidate was asked to make specific commitments to support an agenda which included several elements of Freeman's strategic approach: a commitment to extended day enrichment programs for all children, universal health care, a family wage, long-term job training, affordable housing—the elements necessary to reduce inequality. Imagine that the agenda had been forged through a year-long process of house meetings, small group meetings in churches and in schools, meetings where people's private pain could be transformed into public action. Imagine the new leadership that would be developed through such a process. Imagine the dignity of working people and their families as they collectively forged a powerful role in the governance of their democracy. This campaign of conversation would have created a broad-based constituency with ownership of the agenda, a constituency committed to doing the public business and follow-up work necessary to hold the candidates accountable for their commitments.

A strategy of voter education, registration, and turn-out would ensure that those candidates who committed would be those who were elected. What would happen if, in 2000, at least 75 members of the House of Representatives arrived in Washington with specific mandates from well-organized constituents to reduce the consequences of inequality and declining wages? And what if it were 150 in the year 2002, plus a number of strategically important senators? What would happen if those elected officials had direct experience with an organized group of collective, genuine grassroots leaders in their communities?

I hope that progressives in the academic community will begin to recognize and appreciate the need for broad-based institutional organizing to create the political constituency necessary to carry Richard Freeman's strategies forward. In fact, this is what the IAF organizations are working to create in over 40 communities around the nation. Franklin D. Roosevelt is reported to have said about the need for a specific policy initiative,

"Okay, you've convinced me. Now go out there and organize and create a constituency to make me do it." I fear that too many progressives are still caught up in the "convincing," when what we need now is the constituency—and people who are willing to think hard about how to create, sustain, and energize that constituency.

❧ III ❧

Reply

$\mathcal{T}$he first purpose of my article was to move discussion of the new inequality from analyses of fact or cause or consequence toward developing a sensible long-term plan for improving the economic position of low-wage Americans. In this minimal goal I succeeded. The commentators, some simpatico with the approach I outlined and some not, have clarified the issues in developing a war on inequality.

My second purpose was to begin to lay out a new way to address poverty. The strategies that I proposed are designed to fit naturally with a free-enterprise, market-based economy—to "level the playing field" through asset redistribution, increased opportunity to unionize, or starting-gate equality—while maintaining a modest safety net or social insurance (social wages, appropriately taxed) after that. These strategies sought to encapsulate a basic level of citizen income into private property rights early on to preserve redistributions to the low-income population and minimize interventions with markets. I made cities the focal place for policy initiative for obvious reasons.

I read the responses to this "candidate plan" as falling into two basic categories: some find the five strategies basically right (though they often doubt political feasibility). Others favor more traditional state policies. Tobin, Krugman, Heckman, and Cortes are in the first camp, Piven, Hartmann, and Piore in the second, though all have their own distinct take. The dividing line is whether one puts greater faith in government to address problems or greater faith in individuals and citizen organizations (such as Cortes's IAF), given appropriate initial conditions, to address problems.

To be sure, I agree that there can be no solution to the new inequality without government, just as there can be no property-based capitalism without government enforcing laws. And, to be sure, we need taxes to level the field and give low-income citizens, particularly children, a fair chance in the market economy. And yes, there are good government programs, of which the EITC may be an exemplar, and good training programs. I concur with Jim Heckman that the best training is done early in life—thus, starting-gate equality. But once government accomplishes a basic redistribution, I believe it should step aside and let us all compete fairly in the market (with some modest social insurance for those who fare poorly). Heidi Hartmann encapsulated the disagreement superbly. I believe that most people will prosper in an "ideal virgin capitalism." She fears it will screw us all.

That is a big gap in orientation, though we favor many of the same specific policies.

I am less suspicious than Paul Krugman about the attitudes of conservatives. I have encountered the diehard effort to deny the facts but I have also talked with many businessfolk and political conservatives who recognize that we have a problem and who can and, I hope, will contribute to its solution. When I first began talking explicitly about finding policies to "raise the bottom" of the income distribution through explicit redistribution, even the big liberal foundations thought this an off-base topic. Now there are conservatives willing to enter the conversation.

I am less suspicious of schemes to "privatize social security" than Jim Tobin or most others. Sweden's Social Democrats have enacted a 2 percent mandatory tax for funding pensions above the state level, so Meidner-type plans are not dead. They have to be carefully drawn up and negotiated with the business community, however, and not jammed down anyone's throats. There will be numerous opportunities in the next several years to offer redistributive alternatives to various right-wing schemas. I hope we will take those opportunities and not circle the wagons in defense of Depression Era programs. If we follow Frances Piven's road and don't take the initiative, I fear we are headed toward more and more "welfare reforms."

Everyone says "amen" to unions, but only Michael Piore addressed my scheme to give the right to legislate in this area to the states. I look at public-sector labor law, legislated at the state level, and private-sector law, nationally legislated, and see unions flourishing under the former and dying under the latter. I believe that unions do enough economic and social good that the more pro-union states will succeed in the market. I am dubious that world markets determine all outcomes or that we need world solutions.

Many commentators brought up the critical issue of turning ideas into political and economic reality. In a world where the wealthy own politics, it is hard to imagine things being all that different. But social change occurs discontinuously, and those changes that occur in periods of big change are the lasting ones. When the United States decides to address inequality, we must have available serious plans to turn the big changes into a long-term improvement in the economic position of the low-income citizens. And, yes, we must all try to get the country to face the new inequality honestly, and to create the constituency for it, as Cortes notes.

After reading the commentaries, I still don't think the road to salvation is through old-fashioned welfare state policies, but that something more radical is needed. Some of my conservative friends sometimes call the radical solution citizen capitalism. Some of my left-oriented friends call it propertied socialism. But, as Jim Tobin says, it don't matter what you call it . . . liberalism, conservatism, progressivism, a new New Deal or a new fair deal or whatever tickles your fancy. Let's keep pushing solutions and who knows? If Evander Holyfield can knock out Mike Tyson, the United States can knock out the scourge of the new inequality.

Notes

RICHARD D. FREEMAN / *Solving the New Inequality*
This essay is based on joint work and arguments with Joel Rogers.

1. New Zealand is the leader in *growth* of income inequality, but its inequality remains much below the level here.

2. Richard Freeman, "Toward an Apartheid Economy," *Harvard Business Review* (September–October 1996).

3. The story is the same for job-related benefits; employers continue to provide them to the high skilled and high paid but not so much for the low skilled and low paid. In 1979, 57 percent of male high school graduates had employer-provided pensions; in 1993, 45 percent had employer-provided pensions. In 1979, 78 percent of these high school graduates were covered by employer-provided health insurance; in 1993, 62 percent were covered.

4. Despite the reduced cost of hiring low-skilled workers, their employment and hours worked have fallen relative to that of the better paid. Today, the low paid work less than the high paid, who are putting in many more hours than in the past. One interpretation is that both groups are responding to the rise of inequality; pay the poor less and legitimate work becomes less attractive than crime or welfare; pay the well-to-do more and they become workaholics. This supply interpretation is consistent with the fact that the group with the big increase in jobs are women, whose pay has risen relative to that of men.

5. This is especially so for the $1.5 trillion or so in plans collectively bargained by unions, themselves heavily metropolitan in their base. It will also help preserve and build union strength—a fact that unions themselves increasingly recognize.

6. I caution, though, that I consider this not much more than in-

tuition—more confident claims to the contrary notwithstanding. Sorting out relative life-cycle efficiencies of different sorts of interventions is an important empirical matter, and one of the things that I really do think it makes sense to spend some time and money figuring out.

7. Perhaps reflecting this, those in the bottom parts of the distribution of test scores in the United States fall further below the median than do young persons in the bottom parts of the distribution of test scores in European countries. That the U.S. educational system produces what now seem to be the most unequal outcomes among advanced countries makes a joke of our long-standing snootiness about the alleged class bias of European schooling, and our pretense to classless "comprehensive" schooling here.

8. The Swedish welfare state conditions most benefits to work and has thus encouraged citizens to work. Recent Canadian experience shows that promising welfare recipients sizable lump sum payments when they hold a full-time job for an extended period can alter their behavior toward accepting low-pay jobs that they might otherwise reject in favor of staying on welfare.

9. I do not assume that the wealthy fail to realize that they would be receiving less social income, but that they would recognize that they are covered by the same insurance scheme. Perhaps they might even be getting a more sizable such income when they are young.

10. There are clear, specific proposals that either set of states could follow. The pro-union states could choose to allow workers to organize through card check or through the fast elections the Dunlop commission recommended, or offer arbitration for first contracts, or impose criminal penalties on employers for breaking the labor law. The antiunion states could enact the TEAM Act that Clinton vetoed. Competition would then decide who made the better choice.

James Heckman / *Old Problem, New Despair*

1. John J. Donohue and Peter Siegelman, "Allocating Resources Among Prisons and Social Programs in the Battle Against Crime," working paper, Stanford Law School, 1996, 60–65.

2. See James Heckman, Lance Lochner, Jeffrey Smith, and Chris Taber, "The Effects of Government Policy on Human Capital Investment and Wage Inequality," *Chicago Policy Review* 1, no. 2 (spring 1997): 1–40.

ABOUT THE CONTRIBUTORS

ERNESTO CORTES, JR., is director of the Southwest Industrial Areas Foundation Network and the Texas Interfaith Education Fund. He has been a community organizer for over 20 years.

RICHARD B. FREEMAN holds the Herbert Ascherman Chair of Economics at Harvard University. He is also director of the Labor Studies Program at the National Bureau of Economics Research, and executive director of the Programme in Discontinuous Economics at the London School of Economics' Centre for Economic Performance.

HEIDI HARTMANN is the founder and director of the Institute for Women's Policy Research, a Washington, D.C.–based think tank that focuses on economic issues of special concern to women. An economist with degrees from Swarthmore College and Yale University, she is also a recent recipient of a MacArthur Foundation Fellowship.

JAMES HECKMAN is Henry Schultz Distinguished Professor of Economics at the University of Chicago where he has served since 1973. He holds a parallel appointment as director of social program evaluation at the Harris School of Public Policy at the University of Chicago, and is also senior research fellow at the American Bar Association.

PAUL R. KRUGMAN is professor of economics at the Massachusetts Institute of Technology. His books include *The Age of Diminished Expectations*, *Peddling Prosperity*, and *Pop Internationalism*.

MICHAEL PIORE is David W. Skinner Professor of Political Economy at the Massachusetts Institute of Technology. His latest book is *Beyond Individualism*.

FRANCES FOX PIVEN is on the faculty of the Graduate School of the City University of New York. She is coauthor, with Richard A. Cloward, of *Regulating the Poor*, updated in 1993.

ROBERT B. REICH was secretary of labor during the first Clinton administration. He is University Professor of Social and Economic Policy at Brandeis University's Heller School, and author of seven books, including *Locked in the Cabinet.*

JAMES TOBIN is Sterling Professor of Economics Emeritus at Yale University. In 1961–1962 he was a member of President Kennedy's Council of Economic Advisors.